Thermodynamics and Thermal Physics:

A brief analysis

Md Zaheer Ansari

M.Phil., Ph.D. (IIT-ISM, Dhanbad)
Assistant Professor
School of Basic and Applied Sciences,
Raffles University, Rajasthan

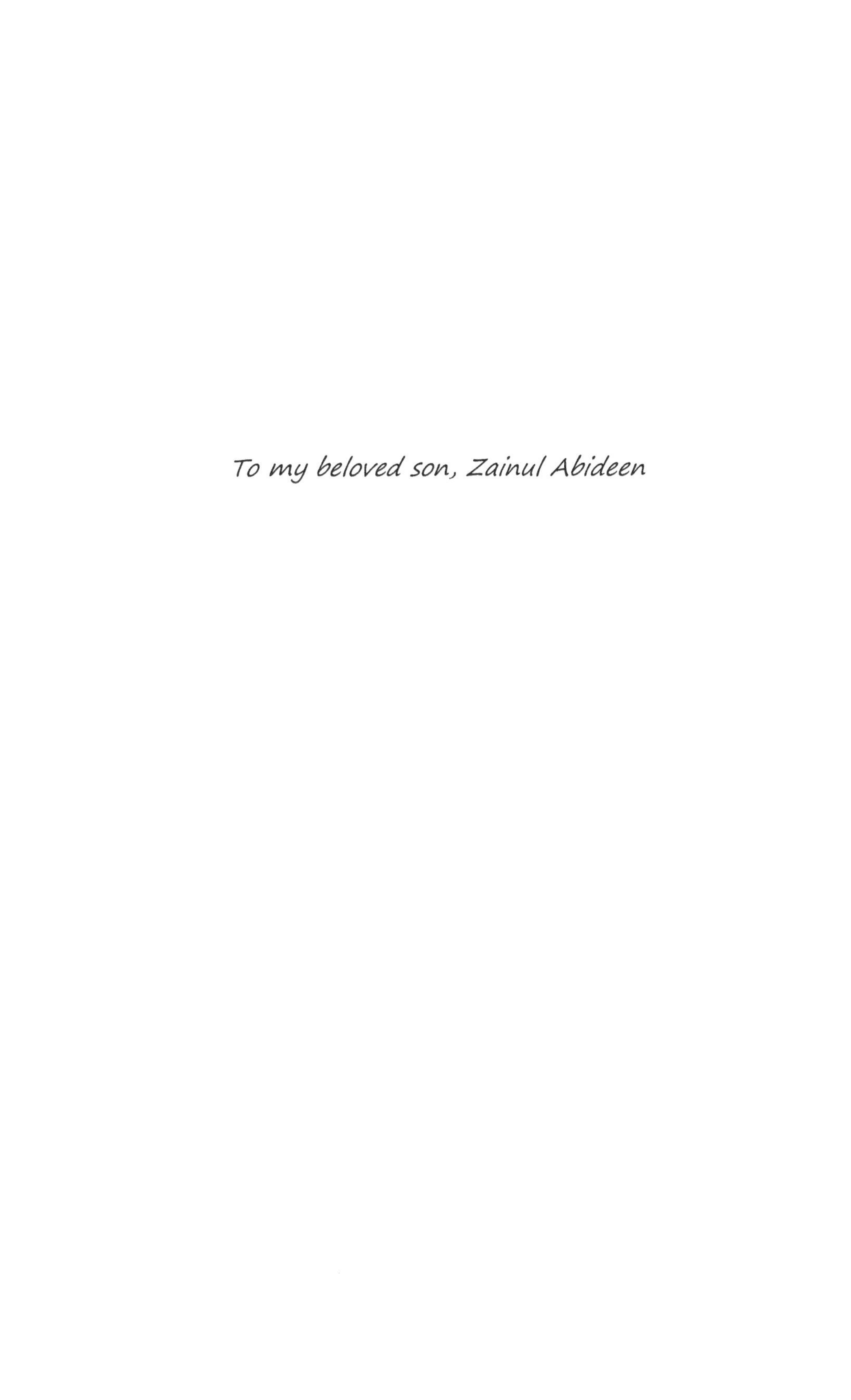

To my beloved son, Zainul Abideen

Preface

This textbook delves into the subject matter of thermodynamics and thermal physics, offering a self-study approach to students and structuring concepts in a cohesive manner.

It includes informative examples and applications to deepen our understanding of these topics. The textbook also presents the essential mathematical methods and tools for explaining theories and concepts.

Designed for both undergraduate and graduate physics and engineering students in Indian universities, this book serves as a valuable reference for integrated graduate courses in physics and photonics.

Rajasthan   MD ZAHEER ANSARI

CONTENTS

Chapter 1
Introduction to thermodynamics

CHAPTER 1.
INTRODUCTION TO THERMODYNAMICS

1.1 Thermodynamic System & Equilibrium

A thermodynamic system can be described with the help of the state variables and their thermodynamic relationship. It also deals with the study of transformations of heat into work and vice versa.

When an isolated system is left alone for a suitable long period of time, it will relax to a state where no further change is noticeable. This state is called equilibrium.

Thermodynamics describe the properties of various macroscopic systems at equilibrium and this can be done with the help of several state variables, such as

- the internal energy (U)
- the volume (V)
- the pressure (P)
- the no. of particles (N)
- the temperature (T)
- the entropy (S)
- the chemical potential (μ)

and others

A state variable can be defined as thermodynamic quantity that depends only on what the state of the system is. These quantities does not dependent on how the system was brought to a particular state. The state variables are not all independent but thermodynamically related .

1.2 Thermodynamic Equilibrium

A system is in equilibrium if its physical properties do not change with time. This signifies that the state variables must be constant in time. Thus a system is in equilibrium if there are no

(1) macroscopic motions (which brings mechanical equilibrium)

(2) macroscopic energy fluxes(which brings thermal equilibrium)

(3) unbalanced phase transitions or chemical reaction (which brings chemical equilibrium)

within the system.

1.2.1 Mechanical equilibrium

The system will be in mechanical equilibrium if the pressure is constant in time & uniform throughout the system.

Explanation : A pressure gradient produces an unbalanced macroscopic force which in turn, brings bulk motion within the system; such a situation does not represent equilibrium.

1.2.2 Thermal equilibrium

Here temperature of the system must be constant in time and uniform throughout the system.

Explanation : If one part of the system is hotter than the other, energy (heat) will flow from that part to the other, again such a situation does not represent equilibrium.

1.2.3 Chemical equilibrium

Here the chemical constant, μ of the system must be constant in time and uniform throughout the system. Thus for the system to be at equilibrium, unbalanced chemical reaction must not occur.

As an example consider the beta decay process, where a proton decays into a neutron, a positron, and a neutrino:

$$p \rightarrow n + e^{+} + \vartheta$$

If the above reaction is unbalanced, the no. of protons in the system will keep on decreasing, while the no. of neutrons, positrons, and neutrinos will keep on increasing. Such a state does not represent equilibrium.

Thus a system which is at once in mechanical, thermal, and chemical equilibrium is said to be in thermodynamic equilibrium.

1.3 Equation of state

The equation of state of a thermodynamic system expresses the fact that not all of its state variables are independent.

Consider a system described by two state variables X and Y, apart from the temperature, T. (for example for an ideal gas, $X \equiv V$, $Y \equiv P$). Now for the system to remain in equilibrium, a given variable X must be accompanied by a specific variation in Y. If Y is not varied by this amount, the system goes out of equilibrium.

Therefore, there must exist an equation of state such that:

$$f(X, Y, T) = 0$$

relating X, Y & T for all equilibrium configurations. For non-equilibrium states:

$$f \neq 0$$

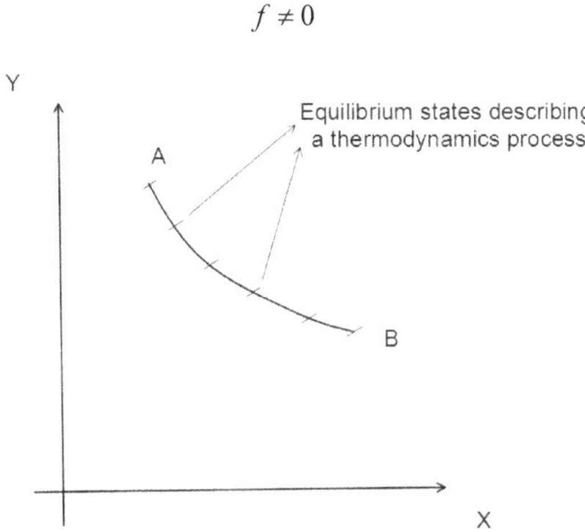

Fig. 1.1 A thermodynamic process undergoing several equilibrium states.

For example, the equation of states of an ideal gas (containing N moles) is

$$f(\text{V, P, T}) = \text{PV} - \text{NKT} = 0$$

Now suppose the system goes from one equilibrium configuration (X,Y,T) to a neighbouring equilibrium state defined by the coordinates $(X + \delta X, Y + \delta Y, T)$ while keeping the temperature constant.

Since both these configurations are at equilibrium, we can define each of the states as follows:

$$f(X,Y,T) = 0$$
$$f(X + \delta X, Y + \delta Y, T) = 0$$

Therefore,

$$f(X+\delta X, Y+\delta Y, T) - f(X,Y,T) = 0$$

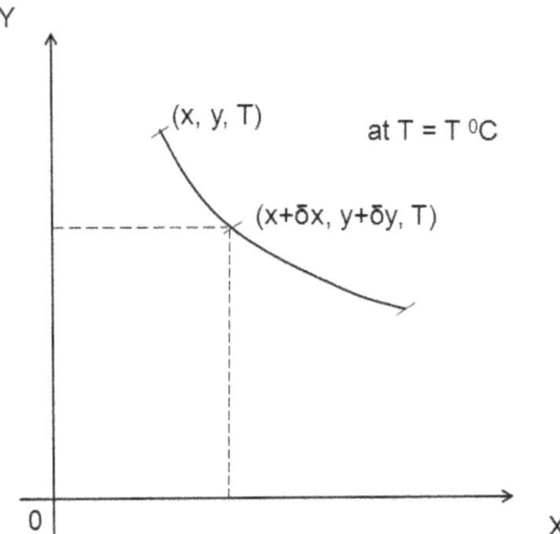

Fig. 1.2 Two equilibrium states describing a thermodynamic process at constant temperature.

Expending the first term as a Taylor's series about (X,Y,T) up to the 1st order, we get:

$$f(x+h) = f(x) + \frac{\partial f(x)}{\partial h} dh$$

$$f(X,Y,T) + \left(\frac{\partial f}{\partial X}\right)_{Y,T} dX + \left(\frac{\partial f}{\partial Y}\right)_{X,T} dY - f(X,Y,T) = 0$$

$$\therefore \quad \left(\frac{\partial f}{\partial X}\right)_{Y,T} dX + \left(\frac{\partial f}{\partial Y}\right)_{X,T} dY = 0$$

Thus X and Y cannot be varied independently if the system is to remain in equilibrium during the transformation.

1.4 Laws of thermodynamics

There are four laws of thermodynamics:

Zeroth Law: It is concerned with the definition of temperature and thermal equilibrium & may be stated as:

" There is a unique scale of temperature."

Then if a body A is in thermal equilibrium with body B, and B with C. Then A is also in thermal equilibrium with C.

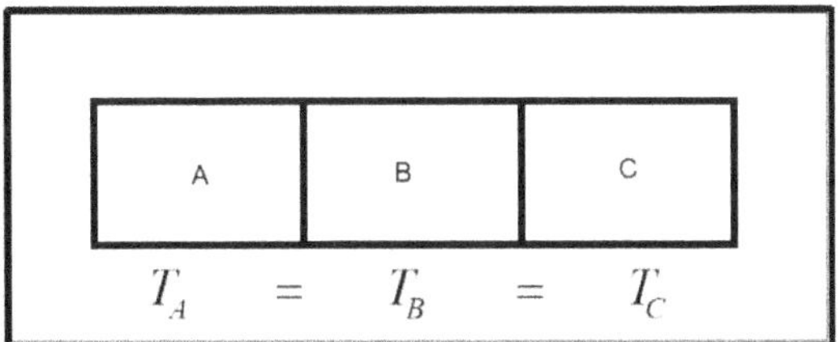

Fig.1.3 Thermal equilibrium

First law : The first law is concerned with the conservation of energy and may be stated as:

"The energy of an isolated system is constant."

This means that energy can neither be created nor destroyed, only transferred between systems, or between a system and its surroundings.

The internal energy U of a system can be increased by either letting the system absorb heat (Q) or doing work (W) on the system. Thus we can write:

$$dU = \partial Q + \partial W$$

Here ∂Q and ∂W are inexact differentials. This means that the integrals $\int_A^B \partial Q$ and $\int_A^B \partial W$ depend not only on the endpoints A and B but also on the path taken to go from A to B. (The path represents the precise way by which the system was taken from state A to B). So Q & W are not state variables. But U is a state variable. That is;

$\int_A^B dU = U(B) - U(A)$ is always valid, independent of the path.

Second law : It is concerned with the spontaneous direction of processes. It can be stated as:

"When two systems are brought into thermal contact, heat flows spontaneously from the one at higher temperature to the one at lower temperature, not the other way round".

There are many equivalent statements of 2nd law such as:

"Heat cannot be completely converted into work for any cyclic process, but work can spontaneously be completely converted into heat".

"Spontaneous changes are always accompanied by a conversion of energy into a more disordered form".

"The entropy S of an isolated system increases during any spontaneous change or process".

Third law: The 3rd law is also concerned with entropy and may be stated as follows:

"All perfect materials have the same entropy S at T= 0, and this value may be taken to be S = 0 at higher temperature, S is always positive. It is impossible to cool any system to T = 0".

1.5 Thermodynamic Systems & Cycles

1.5.1 Reversible transformation

A reversible transformation from state A to state B is one which can be performed equally in the opposite direction (from state B to state A), without introducing any other changes in the thermodynamic system or its surrounding.

Example : Consider the quasi-static compression of a gas. The work done on the system during the compression can be extracted again by letting the gas expand back to its original volume. Since both the gas and the agent are responsible for the compression then return to their original states, the transformation is reversible.

1.5.2 Irreversible transformation

An irreversible transformation from state A to state B is one which can be performed only in this direction; the reversed transformation would introduce additional changes in the system or its surrounding.

Example : Consider the free expansion of a gas caused by the removal of a partition. This transformation is clearly irreversible; replacing the partition once the gas has completely filled the chamber does not make the gas returned back to its original volume.

1.5.3 Cyclic transformation

A cyclic transformation is one which brings the system back to its original state, irrespective of what may happen to the system surroundings. Here the system's final and initial states are one and the same. cyclic transformation can be both reversible and irreversible.

Examples : An example of a reversible cyclic transformation is the quasi-static compression and then re-expansion of a gas.

An irreversible cyclic transformation is the free expansion of a gas followed by a slow compression back to its original volume.

1.6 Clausius theorem and Inequality

The inequality $\oint \dfrac{dQ}{T} \leq 0$ holds for any cyclic transformation. The equality holds if and only if the transformation is reversible. This theorem follows from 2nd law of thermodynamics while inequality is valid for irreversible transformation. Thus,

For a reversible transformation

$$\oint_{R} \frac{\partial Q}{T} = 0$$

The equality sign applies only to the the ideal or Carnot cycle and the integral here shows the net change in entropy in one complete cycle. Thus, for an ideal engine cycle entropy does not decrease.

For an irreversible transformation;

$$\oint_{R} \frac{\partial Q}{T} < 0$$

The Inequality sign applies to any real engine cycle and implies a negative change in entropy on the cycle. So the entropy given to the environment during the cycle is greater than the entropy transferred to the engine by heat from the hot reservoir.

1.7 Thermodynamic system

A system can be characterized by the properties such as T, P, V, composition etc. A thermodynamic system can be the region of chemical interest; e.g: a reaction vessel.

Surroundings : Region outside the system, sometimes where we make our measurements, and separated from the system by a boundary.

1.7.1 Open system

In an open system both energy and matter can be exchanged between the system and its surroundings.

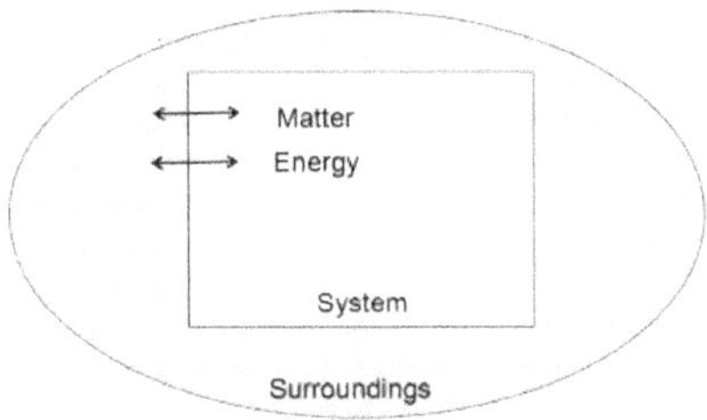

1.7.2 Closed system

In a close system only energy can be transferred either as work or by heat transfer.

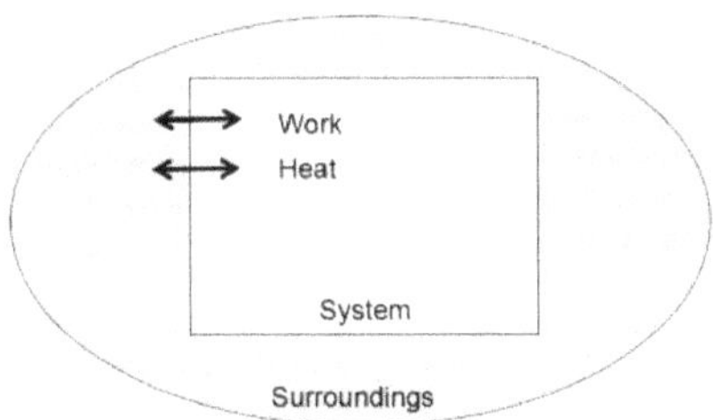

1.7.3 Isolated system

For an isolated system neither energy nor matter can be exchanged between the system and its surroundings.

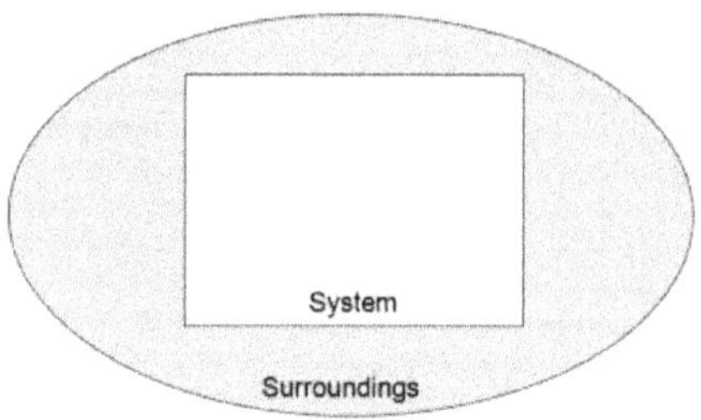

1.7.4 Adiabatic system

The system is thermally isolated, and so heat transfer cannot occur, although work can be performed on or by the system.

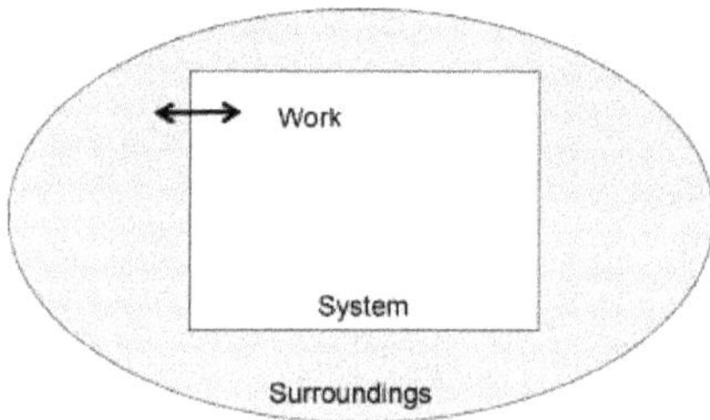

1.7.5 Diathermic system

A system for which heat transfer is possible.

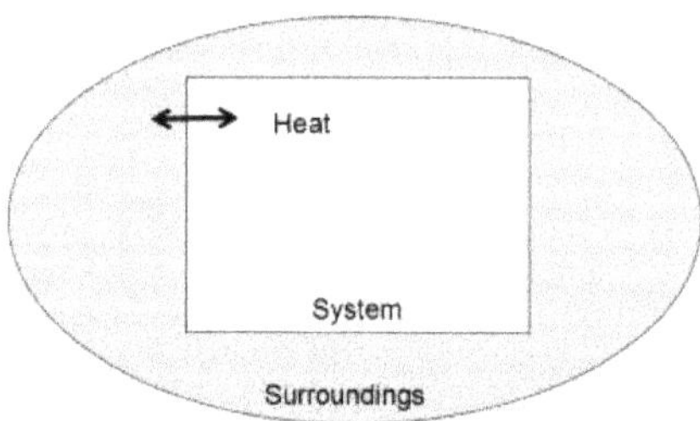

1.8 The internal Energy

The internal energy U of a system is the total energy it contains as a result of its physical state that is under specified condition of P, V, and T etc. According to the first law of thermodynamics, internal energy of a system is constant unless it is changed by work, W or by heat transfer Q :

$$\Delta U = W + Q$$

[A large macroscopic change in a quantity x is Δx while a small incremental change of x is dx.]

The internal energy, U is a state function as it does not depend on how that state was reached. The value of U depend on the amount of matter in the system. If we double the mass, we double U. In microscopic terms (i.e; at the molecular level), U is equal to the total sum of the energy levels of the atoms or molecules making up the system, weighted by their probabilities of being occupied.

1.9 Extensive and Intensive Variables

The equilibrium state of a thermodynamic system at a particular time is described by a set of state functions called properties. State functions do not depend on how that state was reached.

Intensive properties such as temperature, pressure, & density do not depend on the size, mass or configuration of the system. Intensive properties have meaning only when the system is in equilibrium or for systems in equilibrium states.

The properties that depend on the size of the system, such as length, volume, mass and energy are called extensive properties.

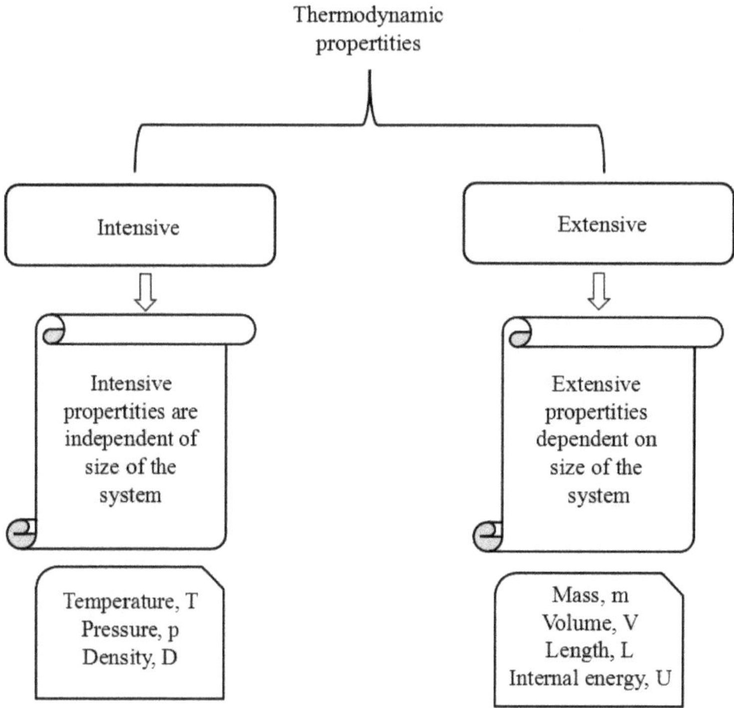

Fig. 1.4 Extensive and Intensive Variables.

The ratio of two extensive properties of a homogeneous system defines an intensive properties. Mass per unit volume is an intensive property.

1.10 Thermodynamic processes & cycles

A process is the path followed by a system as it undergoes a change of state. A process can be described by the successive thermodynamic states through which the system passes.

Consider an ideal or quasi-equilibrium process in which the state of the system deviates from thermodynamic equilibrium by only infinitesimal amount throughout the entire process.

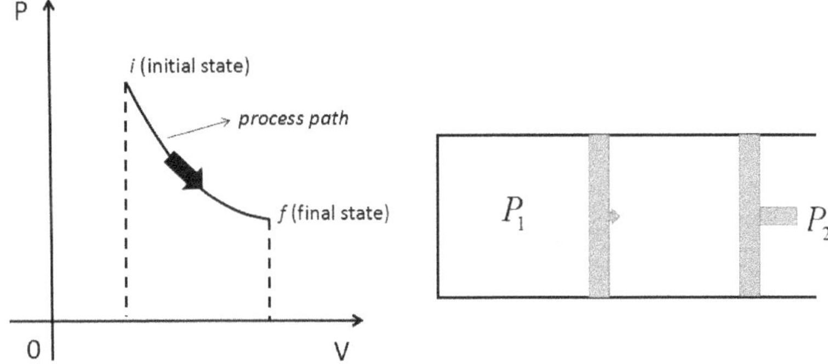

Fig. 1.5 (a) A thermodynamic process, and (b) the process of expansion.

(a) If $P_1 = P_2$, the piston is in equilibrium.

(b) If $P_1 > P_2$ (infinitesimal increment), the gas will undergo an expansion.

During the process energy transfer may take place at the system boundary (by heat or by work) & changes in properties of the system may occur.

Those properties or phenomena that do not change during a process can be used to describe the system.

1.10.1 Thermodynamic Cycle

When a system at a given initial state undergoes a sequence of processes and then returns back to its original state, the system is said to be completed a thermodynamic cycle.

Thus the properties of the system at the completion of the cycle remains same as those at the initial state.

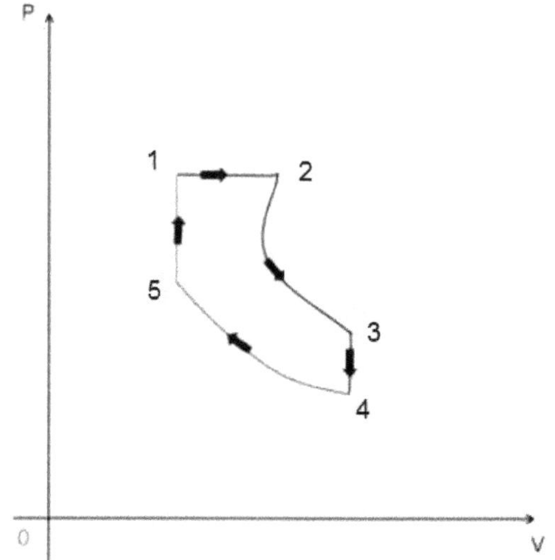

Fig. 1.6 P-V diagram of a thermodynamic cycle.

Chapter 2
Thermodynamics and Entropy

CHAPTER 2.

THERMODYNAMICS AND ENTROPY

2.1 Entropy

Consider a thermodynamic system described by the two equilibrium states i and f. Since i and f are equilibrium states, number of different reversible paths may be used to take the system from i to f.

Suppose the system is taken from i to f along the reversible path R_1 and then back to i along the reversible path R_2 .

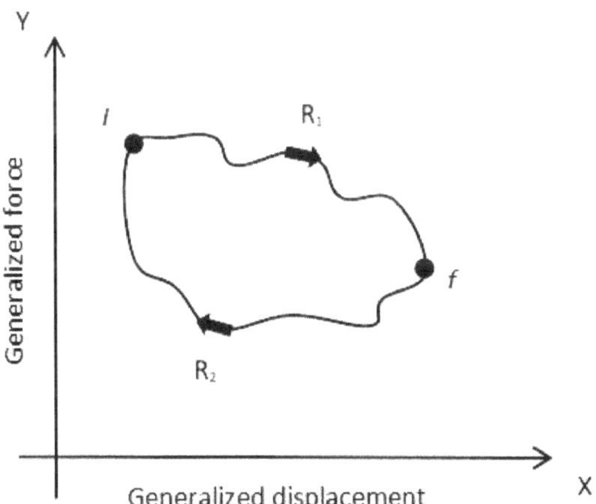

Fig. 2.1 Two reversible paths connecting two equilibrium states of a system.

The two paths form a reversible cycle, therefore we can write from the Clausius theorem,

$$\oint_{R_1 R_2} \frac{dQ}{T} = 0$$

$$or, \quad \int_{R_1 \ i}^{f} \frac{dQ}{T} + \int_{R_2 \ f}^{i} \frac{dQ}{T} = 0$$

$$or, \quad \int_{R_1 \ i}^{f} \frac{dQ}{T} = - \int_{R_2 \ f}^{i} \frac{dQ}{T}$$

$$or, \quad \int_{R_1 \ i}^{f} \frac{dQ}{T} = \int_{R_2 \ i}^{f} \frac{dQ}{T} \tag{1}$$

Thus we have,

$$\int_{R \ i}^{f} \frac{dQ}{T} = \text{constant}$$

$$\therefore \quad \int_{R \ i}^{f} \frac{dQ}{T} \text{ is independant of path.}$$

Let
$$\frac{dQ}{T} = dS \tag{2}$$

$$\therefore \quad \int_{i}^{f} dS = \int_{i}^{f} \frac{dQ}{T}$$

or,
$$S_f - S_i = \int_{i}^{f} \frac{dQ}{T} \tag{3}$$

Then there exist a function of thermodynamic coordinates of a system whose value at the final state minus its value at initial state equals the integral $\int_{R \ i}^{f} \frac{dQ}{T}$. This state function is called entropy & denoted by S.

Therefore a finite change in entropy $S_f - S_i$ from state i to f is

$$S_f - S_i = \int\limits_{R\,i}^{f} \frac{dQ}{T}$$

If the equilibrium states i & f are infinitesimally near, the integration may be eliminated & $S_f - S_i$ becomes dS, an infinitesimal change of entropy.

$$\therefore \quad dS = \frac{\partial Q_R}{T} \tag{4}$$

2.2 Entropy and first law of thermodynamics

Consider an ideal gas as a system. Form first law of thermodynamics, we have

$$dQ = dU + PdV$$

Heat capacity at constant volume is given by,

$$C_V = \left(\frac{dQ}{\partial T}\right)_V = \left(\frac{dU}{\partial T}\right)_V$$

But for an ideal gas, U is a function of T only,

$$C_V = \frac{dU}{\partial T} \quad or, \quad C_V dT = dU$$

Thus, $\qquad\qquad dQ = C_V dT + PdV \tag{5}$

Now all equilibrium states can be represented by the ideal gas equation:

$$PV = nRT$$

And for an infinitesimal quasi-static process:

$$PdV + VdP = nRdT$$

Substituting the above expression into equation (5), we get

$$dQ = C_V dT + nRdT - VdP$$

$$dQ = \left(C_V + nR\right)dT - VdP \tag{6}$$

or,

$$\frac{dQ}{dT} = \left(C_V + nR\right) - V\frac{dP}{dT}$$

at constant pressure,

$$\frac{dQ}{dT} = C_P \ \& \ dP = 0$$

$$\therefore \qquad C_P = C_V + nR \quad (ideal\ gas) \tag{7}$$

Similarly from (6)

$$dQ = \left(C_V + nR\right)dT - VdP$$

$$dQ = C_P dT - VdP \tag{8}$$

2.3 Entropy of ideal gas

2.3.1 *Change of Entropy of the ideal gas as a function of T and P:*

Consider a system absorbs an infinitesimal amount of heat dQ_R during a reversible process, the entropy change of the system is

$$dS = \frac{dQ_R}{T}$$

Here dQ_R represents an inexact differential. However the ratio $\frac{dQ_R}{T}$ is exact. Now for an ideal gas, we have the following expression for dQ_R

$$dQ_R = C_P dT - VdP$$

Dividing by T, we get

$$\frac{dQ_R}{T} = C_P \frac{dT}{T} - \frac{V}{T} dP$$

$$or, \quad dS = C_P \frac{dT}{T} - nR \frac{dP}{P} \tag{9}$$

$$\because PV = nRT$$
$$or, \frac{V}{T} = \frac{nR}{P}$$

Now if the system (ideal gas) undergoes from a reference start $r(T_r, P_r)$ to a state defined by the coordinates (T, P), integrating between these two states, we get

$$S - S_r = \Delta S = \int_{T_r}^{T} C_P \frac{dT}{T} - nR \int_{P_r}^{P} \frac{dP}{P}$$

$$S - S_r = \Delta S = \int_{T_r}^{T} C_P \frac{dT}{T} - nR \ln \frac{P}{P_r}$$

If C_p is constant

$$S - S_r = C_P \ln \frac{T}{T_r} - nR \ln \frac{P}{P_r}$$

or, $\qquad S - S_r = C_P \ln T - C_P \ln T_r - nR \ln P + nR \ln P_r$

or, $\qquad S = C_P \ln T - nR \ln P + \left(S_r - C_P \ln T_r + nR \ln P_r\right)$

or, $\qquad S = C_P \ln T - nR \ln P + S_0$

where

$$S_0 = S_r - C_P \ln T_r + nR \ln P_r \tag{10}$$

in terms of T & P.

The reference state is arbitrarily chosen. For most of the chemical reactions $P_r = 0.1$ Mpa and $T_r = 25°C$ (298 K) is taken as reference state; in engineering the triple point of water for steam process is chosen as reference state; and physicists use 0.1 Mpa and absolute zero for low temperature calculations.

2.3.2 *Change of Entropy of ideal gas as a function of T and V:*

From first law thermodynamics and Eq. (5), we have

$$dQ = C_v dT + P dV$$

or,
$$\frac{dQ}{T} = C_v \frac{dT}{T} + \frac{P}{T} dV$$

or,
$$dS = C_v \frac{dT}{T} + nR \frac{dV}{V}$$

Integrating, we obtain

$$S = \int C_v \frac{dT}{T} + nR \ln V + S_0 \tag{11}$$

In terms of molar specific heat at constant volume C_V, the change of entropy of the ideal gas between an initial states and final state is given by,

$$\Delta S = n \int_i^f c_v \frac{dT}{T} + nR \ln \frac{V_f}{V_i} \tag{12}$$

$$\left[\because c_v = \frac{C_V}{n}, C_V = nc_v \right]$$

Similarly change of entropy of an ideal gas as a function of T and P can be calculated out

$$\Delta S = n\int_{i}^{f} c_{P}\, \frac{dT}{T} - nR \ln \frac{P_{f}}{P_{i}} \tag{13}$$

where c_{P} is the molar specific heat at constant pressure.

2.4 Temperature – Entropy diagram (TS diagram)

Consider a reversible process. Let an infinitesimal amount of heat dQ enters the system,

We have,

$$dQ_{R} = TdS$$

Therefore, the total amount of heat transferred (to the system) in a reversible process from the state i to the state f is given by

$$Q_{R} = \int_{i}^{f} TdS \tag{14}$$

This integral can be interpreted graphically as the area under a curve on a diagram in which T is plotted along the y-axis and S along the x-axis. This diagram is called **TS** diagram.

The shape of the curve on the TS diagram can be determined by the kind of reversible process that the system undergoes. An isothermal process will be a horizontal line.

In the case of reversible adiabatic process, we have ,

$$dS = \frac{dQ_{R}}{T}$$

Also, for an adiabatic process

$$dQ = 0$$

So if T is not zero, then

$$dS = 0$$

$$S = \text{constant}$$

"*Thus during a reversible adiabatic process, the entropy of a system remains constant.*" On the other hand one can say that the system undergoes an isentropic process.

An isentropic process on a TS diagram is a vertical line and called isentrope. Two isothermal and the two adiabatic processes that make up any Carnot cycle is a rectangle on a TS diagram.

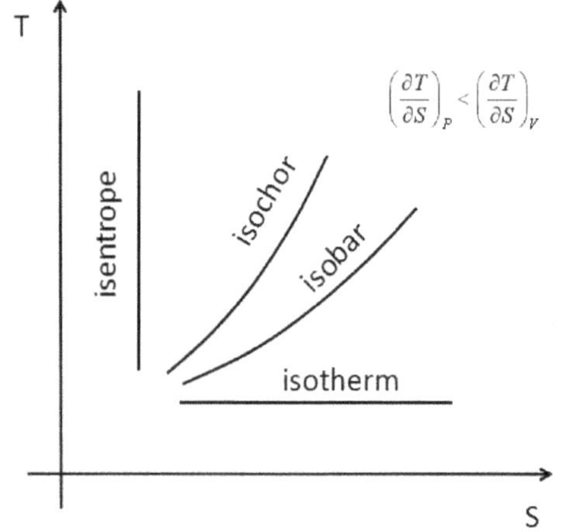

Fig 2.2. Several reversible processes on Temperature-Entropy diagram.

For a reversible isobaric process

$$\left(\frac{\partial T}{\partial S}\right)_P = \frac{T}{C_P} \tag{15}$$

$$\left[\because dS = C_P\,\frac{dT}{T} - nR\,\frac{dP}{P};\ at\ P = \text{constant},\ dS = C_P\,\frac{dT}{T}\right.$$

$$\left. or,\ \left(\frac{\partial T}{\partial S}\right)_P = \frac{T}{C_P}\right]$$

The curve has a slope that follows from Eq. (15) at constant P.

Similarly for constant volume, one can obtain

$$\left(\frac{\partial T}{\partial S}\right)_V = \frac{T}{C_V} \tag{16}$$

$$\left[\because dS = C_V\,\frac{dT}{T} + nR\,\frac{dV}{V};\ at\ \text{constant},\ V,\ \left(\frac{\partial T}{\partial S}\right)_V = \frac{T}{C_V}\right]$$

$$\therefore \left(\frac{\partial T}{\partial S}\right)_P < \left(\frac{\partial T}{\partial S}\right)_V$$

2.5 Entropy and 2nd law of thermodynamics: Clausius theorem

For any cyclic transformation, the entropy of a system follow the inequality $\oint \frac{dQ}{T} \leq 0$. This theorem follows from 2nd law of thermodynamics.

For a reversible transformation

$$\oint_R \frac{\partial Q}{T} = 0$$

The equality sign applies only to the the ideal or Carnot cycle and the integral here shows the net change in entropy in one complete cycle. Thus, for an ideal engine cycle entropy does not decrease.

For an irreversible transformation

$$\oint_R \frac{\partial Q}{T} < 0$$

The Inequality sign applies to any real engine cycle and implies a negative change in entropy on the cycle. So the entropy given to the environment during the cycle is greater than the entropy transferred to the engine by heat from the hot reservoir.

2.6 Efficiency of Carnot engine

The Carnot cycle makes an engine and is composed of two isothermal lines and two adiabatic lines. Fig 2.3 presents the pV and ST diagrams showing the operation of a Carnot engine, where the "working fluid" is an ideal gas.

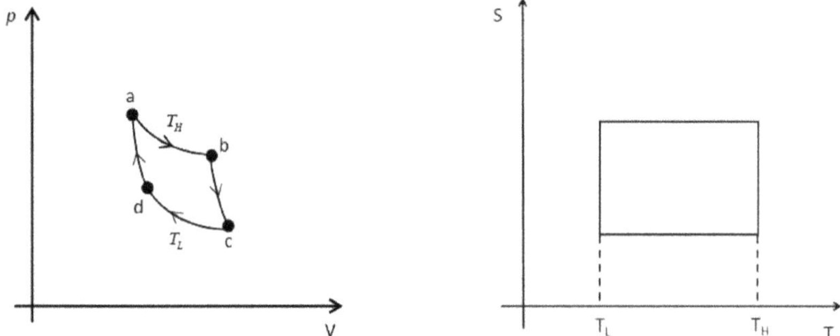

Fig 2.3. The operation of a Carnot engine on the pV and ST diagrams.

The T_H and T_L are the temperatures as measured on an ideal gas thermometer.

$$T = \frac{pV}{NR}$$

One cycle of the Carnot engine acts as follows:

Path a to b describes an isothermal expansion at high temperature T_H . As the gas expands, it does work $|W_1|$. Expansion normally sends the temperature down. To keep the same temperature, the gas must absorb heat $|Q_1|$ from its surroundings.

Path b to c describes an adiabatic expansion. As the gas expands, it does work $|W_2|$. The expansion sends the temperature down. Because the process is adiabatic, no heat is absorbed or ejected.

Path c to d describes an isothermal compression at low temperature T_L. As the gas contracts, work $|W_3|$ is done on the gas. Compression normally sends the temperature up. To keep the same temperature, the gas must eject heat $|Q_2|$ into its surroundings.

Path d to a describes an adiabatic compression. As the gas contracts, work $|W_4|$ is done on the gas. The compression sends the temperature up. Because it's adiabatic, no heat is absorbed or ejected.

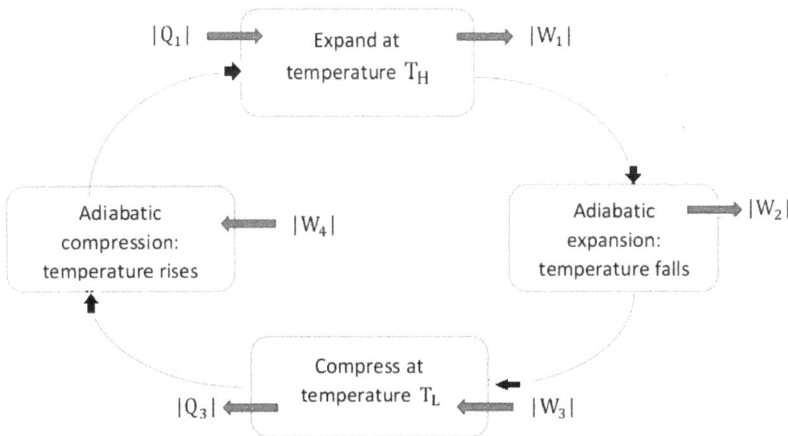

Fig 2.4. Working cycles of an ideal Carnot engine.

During the whole cycle, the gas absorbs some heat and eject some heat as well as gas does some work and some work is done on it. Thus the efficiency of the engine can be calculated out:

$$\text{efficiency} = \frac{\text{net work done by gas}}{\text{heat absorbed by gas}} = \frac{|W_1| + |W_2| - |W_3| - |W_4|}{|Q_1|} \tag{17}$$

If the gas is considered at equilibrium while the volume is changing, the work done by a quasi-static fluid is

$$\int p(V)dV$$

Process a to b: On isothermal expansion, the temperature is T_H so

$$p(V) = \frac{NRT_H}{V} \tag{18}$$

The work done by the gas is then

$$\begin{aligned}
W_1 &= \int_a^b p(V)dV \\
&= \int_a^b \frac{NRT_H}{V} dV \\
&= NRT_H \int_a^b \frac{dV}{V} \\
&= NRT_H \left[ln\,(V) \right]_a^b \\
&= NRT_H \; ln\frac{V_b}{V_a} \tag{19}
\end{aligned}$$

As the system undergoes an expansion, $V_b > V_a$, so this quantity is positive. The energy of a given sample of an ideal gas is a function of temperature alone and so the heat absorbed merely counteracts the effect of the work done, so

$$|Q_1| = |W_1| \tag{20}$$

Process b to c: On adiabatic expansion, the pressure and volume are related through

$$pV^\gamma = constant = p_b V_b^\gamma = p_c V_c^\gamma \tag{21}$$

since,
$$p_b V_b^\gamma = p_c V_c^\gamma$$

$$p_b V_b V_b^{\gamma-1} = p_c V_c V_c^{\gamma-1}$$

$$NRT_H V_b^{\gamma-1} = NRT_L V_c^{\gamma-1}$$

$$\frac{T_H}{T_L} = \left(\frac{V_c}{V_b}\right)^{\gamma-1} \tag{22}$$

An increase in volume will result in a decrease in temperature (for example, in releasing air from a bicycle tire), the work done by the gas can calculated out as:

$$W_2 = \int_b^c p(V)dV$$

$$= constant \int_b^c \frac{1}{V^\gamma} dV$$

$$= constant \left[\frac{1}{-\gamma+1} V^{(-\gamma+1)}\right]_b^c$$

$$= \frac{1}{-\gamma+1}\left[\frac{constant}{V_c^{\gamma-1}} - \frac{constant}{V_b^{\gamma-1}}\right]$$

$$= \frac{1}{-\gamma+1}\left[\frac{p_c V_c^\gamma}{V_c^{\gamma-1}} - \frac{p_b V_b^\gamma}{V_b^{\gamma-1}}\right]$$

$$= \frac{1}{-\gamma+1}[p_c V_c - p_b V_b]$$

$$= \frac{1}{-\gamma+1} NR[T_L - T_H]$$

$$= \frac{NR}{1-\gamma}(T_H - T_L) \tag{23}$$

Again, this quantity is positive.

Path c to d: In the isothermal compression, work done by the gas is calculated similar to equation (19).

$$W_3 = NRT_L ln \frac{V_d}{V_c}. \tag{24}$$

Because $V_d < V_c$, the work done by the gas is negative. The work done on the gas is

$$|W_3| = - NRT_L ln\frac{V_d}{V_c} = NRT_L ln\frac{V_c}{V_d} \tag{25}$$

Again,

$$|Q_3| = |W_3| \tag{26}$$

Path d to a: There is adiabatic compression and the calculations are similar to equations (22) and (23). We have

$$\frac{T_L}{T_H} = \left(\frac{V_a}{V_d}\right)^{\gamma-1} \tag{27}$$

And

$$W_4 = \frac{NR}{\gamma-1}(T_L - T_H) \tag{28}$$

As expected, this quantity is negative and

$$|W_4| = - W_4 = \frac{NR}{\gamma-1}(T_H - T_L) \tag{29}$$

Thus the efficiency of engine is

$$\eta = \frac{|W_1| + |W_2| - |W_3| - |W_4|}{|Q_1|}$$

$$= 1 + \frac{|W_2| - |W_3| - |W_4|}{|Q_1|}$$

One can show that $|W_2| = |W_4|$. Using the values for $|W_3|$ and Q_1, we find

$$\eta = 1 - \frac{|W_3|}{|Q_1|} = 1 - \frac{NRT_L \, ln\,(V_c/V_d)}{NRT_H \, ln\,(V_b/V_a)}$$

$$= 1 - \frac{T_L \, ln\,(V_c/V_d)}{T_H \, ln\,(V_b/V_a)}$$

Comparing equation (22) and (27), we find

$$\frac{T_H}{T_L} = \left(\frac{V_c}{V_b}\right)^{\gamma-1} = \left(\frac{V_d}{V_a}\right)^{\gamma-1}$$

so
$$\frac{V_c}{V_b} = \frac{V_d}{V_a}$$

or
$$\frac{V_c}{V_d} = \frac{V_b}{V_a}$$

Thus, the efficiency of an ideal Carnot engine with ideal gas as a working substance is given by

$$\eta = 1 - \frac{T_L}{T_H} \tag{30}$$

The efficiency is independent of the volume and depends only on the two temperatures concerned. The above equation is derived for a reversible Carnot engine (or the cycle). However, if the engine is not reversible, its efficiency is

$$\eta < \eta'$$

Chapter 3. Thermodynamic functions and their relationship

CHAPTER 3.
THERMODYNAMIC FUNCTIONS AND THEIR RELATIONSHIP

3.1 Thermodynamic work done

There are many ways of doing work on a thermodynamic system. one of the ways is to compress (or decompress) the system.

As shown in the fig., work done during a displacement dx is

$$dW = Fdx =- PAdx =- P(Adx)$$

where A being area of the piston.

Thus $\quad dW =- PdV$

(1) The work done during a compression is positive.

(2) Work done is negative during an expansion

Another way of doing work is to inject new particles into the system. In that case

$$dW \propto dN$$

$$dW_{injection} = \mu dN$$

μ is the constant of proportionality. It is depend as injection energy per particle.

i.e, $\qquad \mu = \dfrac{dW}{dN}$

3.2 Thermodynamic potentials

For a reversible transformation, we have

$$\mathit{d}Q = TdS$$

3.2.1. *Energy*

For a reversible transformations, the 1st law of thermodynamics states

$$dE = \mathit{d}Q + \mathit{d}W$$

$$dE = TdS - PdV + \mu dN \tag{1}$$

Mathematically, we can write

$$E = E(S, V, N)$$

$$dE = \left(\frac{\partial E}{\partial S}\right)_{V,N} dS + \left(\frac{\partial E}{\partial V}\right)_{S,N} dV + \left(\frac{\partial E}{\partial N}\right)_{V,S} dN \tag{2}$$

comparing equations (1) and (2), we get the definition of T, P and μ as

$$T = \left(\frac{\partial E}{\partial S}\right)_{V,N}$$

$$P = -\left(\frac{\partial E}{\partial V}\right)_{S,N}$$

$$\mu = \left(\frac{\partial E}{\partial N}\right)_{S,V}$$

Thus from E=E(S,V,N), we have the following interpretations:

"S, V, N can be considered as independent variables and that E is a dependent quantity. T, P and μ are also dependent quantities".

3.2.2 *Enthalpy*

Enthalpy of a thermodynamic system can be defined as

$$H = E + PV$$

For a reversible infinitesimal change, we have

$$dH = dE + PdV + VdP \tag{3}$$

From equation (1), we have

$$dE = TdS - PdV + \mu dN$$

Therefore, $\qquad dH - PdV - VdP = TdS - PdV + \mu dN$

or, $\qquad dH = TdS + VdP + \mu dN$

$\therefore \qquad H = H(S,P,N)$

$$dH = \left(\frac{\partial H}{\partial S}\right)_{P,N} dS + \left(\frac{\partial H}{\partial P}\right)_{S,N} dP + \left(\frac{\partial H}{\partial N}\right)_{S,P} dN$$

On comparing, we get

$$T = \left(\frac{\partial H}{\partial S}\right)_{P,N}$$

$$V = \left(\frac{\partial H}{\partial P}\right)_{S,N}$$

$$\mu = \left(\frac{\partial H}{\partial N}\right)_{S,P}$$

3.2.3 *Helmholtz free energy*

Helmholtz free energy of a system can be defined as

$$F = E - TS \tag{4}$$

$$dF = dE - TdS - SdT$$

But from equation (1)

$$dE=TdS-PdV+\mu dN$$

$$dF+TdS+SdT= TdS-PdV+\mu dN$$

$$dF= -SdT-PdV+\mu dN$$

Thus
$$F = F(T,V,N)$$

$$\therefore \quad dF = \left(\frac{\partial F}{\partial T}\right)_{V,N} dT + \left(\frac{\partial F}{\partial V}\right)_{T,N} dV + \left(\frac{\partial F}{\partial N}\right)_{T,V} dN$$

On comparing, we get

$$S =- \left(\frac{\partial F}{\partial T}\right)_{V,N},$$

$$P =- \left(\frac{\partial F}{\partial V}\right)_{T,N}, \text{ and}$$

$$\mu = \left(\frac{\partial F}{\partial N}\right)_{T,V}$$

3.2.4. *Gibbs free energy*

We define the Gibbs free energy as

$$G=E-TS+PV \tag{5}$$

For a differential change, we get

$$dG=dE-TdS-SdT+PdV+VdP$$

But from equation (1)

$$dE=TdS-PdV+\mu dN$$

or, $\quad dG+TdS+SdT-PdV-VdP=TdS-PdV+\mu dN$

or, $dG = -SdT + VdP + \mu dN$

Thus we define

$$G = G(T,P,N)$$

$$\therefore \quad dG = \left(\frac{\partial G}{\partial T}\right)_{P,N} dT + \left(\frac{\partial G}{\partial P}\right)_{T,N} dP + \left(\frac{\partial G}{\partial N}\right)_{T,P} dN$$

On comparing, we get

$$S = -\left(\frac{\partial G}{\partial T}\right)_{P,N},$$

$$V = \left(\frac{\partial G}{\partial P}\right)_{T,N} \text{ and}$$

$$\mu = \left(\frac{\partial G}{\partial N}\right)_{T,P}$$

3.3 Maxwell's thermodynamic relations

The definitions for T, S, V, P, μ and N in terms of the thermodynamic potential's E, H, F, G and Ω can be used to generate many relations between the various derivatives of these quantities.

From first law, we have

$$dE = TdS - PdV + \mu dN$$

$$\therefore \quad E = E(S,V,N)$$

$$\therefore \quad dE = \left(\frac{\partial E}{\partial S}\right)_{V,N} dS + \left(\frac{\partial E}{\partial V}\right)_{S,N} dV + \left(\frac{\partial E}{\partial N}\right)_{S,V} dN$$

On comparing, we get

$$T = \left(\frac{\partial E}{\partial S}\right)_{V,N}$$

$$P = -\left(\frac{\partial E}{\partial V}\right)_{S,N}$$

Thus

$$\left(\frac{\partial T}{\partial V}\right)_{S,N} = \left(\frac{\partial^2 E}{\partial V \partial S}\right)$$

and
$$\left(\frac{\partial P}{\partial S}\right)_{V,N} = -\left(\frac{\partial^2 E}{\partial V \partial S}\right)$$

$\therefore$
$$\left(\frac{\partial T}{\partial V}\right)_{S,N} = \left(\frac{\partial^2 E}{\partial S \partial V}\right) = -\left(\frac{\partial P}{\partial S}\right)_{V,N} \tag{6a}$$

Equation (6) is known as Maxwell's first thermodynamic relations. Other relations can be derived from other thermodynamic potentials.

$$\left(\frac{\partial T}{\partial P}\right)_{S,N} = \left(\frac{\partial V}{\partial S}\right)_{P,N} \tag{6b}$$

$$\left(\frac{\partial S}{\partial V}\right)_{T,N} = \left(\frac{\partial P}{\partial T}\right)_{V,N} \tag{6c}$$

$$\left(\frac{\partial S}{\partial P}\right)_{T,N} = -\left(\frac{\partial V}{\partial T}\right)_{P,N} \tag{6d}$$

These four relations are known as Maxwell's thermodynamic relations. These relations hold for any thermodynamic system.

3.3.1 Maxwell's Second relation: *The enthalpy*

$$H = E + PV$$

$$dH = dE + PdV + VdP$$

From 1st law of thermodynamics,

$$dE = TdS - PdV + \mu dN$$

Thus, we get

$$dH - PdV - VdP = TdS - PdV + \mu dN$$

$$dH = TdS + VdP + \mu dN$$

Therefore, $\quad H=H(S,P,N)$

and
$$dH = \left(\frac{\partial H}{\partial S}\right)_{P,N} dS + \left(\frac{\partial H}{\partial P}\right)_{S,N} dP + \left(\frac{\partial H}{\partial N}\right)_{S,P} dN$$

Thus on comparing we get,

$$T = \left(\frac{\partial H}{\partial S}\right)_{P,N}$$

$$V = \left(\frac{\partial H}{\partial P}\right)_{S,N}$$

Thereby,

$$\left(\frac{\partial T}{\partial P}\right)_{S,N} = \left(\frac{\partial^2 H}{\partial P \partial S}\right)$$

$$\left(\frac{\partial V}{\partial S}\right)_{P,N} = \left(\frac{\partial^2 H}{\partial P \partial S}\right)$$

$$\left(\frac{\partial T}{\partial P}\right)_{S,N} = \left(\frac{\partial V}{\partial S}\right)_{P,N}$$

3.3.2 Third relation: *Helmholtz free energy functions*

We have,

$$F = E\text{-}TS$$

$$dF = dE\text{-}TdS\text{-}SdT$$

but from 1st law,

$$dE = TdS\text{-}PdV + \mu dN$$

$$dF + TdS + SdT = TdS\text{-}PdV + \mu dN$$

$$dF = \text{-}SdT\text{-}PdV + \mu dN$$

$\therefore \qquad F = F(T,V,N)$

and

$$dF = \left(\frac{\partial F}{\partial T}\right)_{V,N} dT + \left(\frac{\partial F}{\partial V}\right)_{T,N} dV + \left(\frac{\partial F}{\partial N}\right)_{T,V} dN$$

On comparing the above equations, we get

$$S = -\left(\frac{\partial F}{\partial T}\right)_{V,N}$$

$$P = -\left(\frac{\partial F}{\partial V}\right)_{T,N}$$

and

$$\left(\frac{\partial S}{\partial V}\right)_{T,N} = -\left(\frac{\partial^2 F}{\partial V \partial T}\right)$$

$$\left(\frac{\partial P}{\partial T}\right)_{V,N} = -\left(\frac{\partial^2 F}{\partial T \partial V}\right)$$

Thus

$$\left(\frac{\partial S}{\partial V}\right)_{T,N} = \left(\frac{\partial P}{\partial T}\right)_{V,N}$$

3.3.3 Fourth relation: Gibbs free energy function

we have,

$$G = E - TS + PV$$

$$dG = dE - TdS - SdT + PdV + VdP$$

but from 1st law,

$$dE = TdS - PdV + \mu dN$$

$$dG + TdS + SdT - PdV - VdP = TdS - PdV + \mu dN$$

$$dG = -SdT + VdP + \mu dN$$

$\therefore \qquad\qquad G = G(T,P,N)$

and $\qquad dG = \left(\frac{\partial G}{\partial T}\right)_{P,N} dT + \left(\frac{\partial G}{\partial P}\right)_{T,N} dP + \left(\frac{\partial G}{\partial N}\right)_{T,P} dN$

while comparing, we get

$$S = -\left(\frac{\partial G}{\partial T}\right)_{P,N}$$

$$V = \left(\frac{\partial G}{\partial P}\right)_{T,N}$$

And

$$\left(\frac{\partial S}{\partial P}\right)_{T,N} = -\left(\frac{\partial^2 G}{\partial P \partial T}\right)$$

$$\left(\frac{\partial V}{\partial T}\right)_{P,N} = \left(\frac{\partial^2 G}{\partial T \partial P}\right)$$

Therefore,

$$\left(\frac{\partial S}{\partial P}\right)_{T,N} = -\left(\frac{\partial V}{\partial T}\right)_{P,N}$$

3.4 Gibbs-Helmholtz equation: Pressure and temperature dependence of Gibbs function

For an isothermal process, we can obtain (see section 3.2.4)

$$V = \left(\frac{\partial G}{\partial P}\right)_T \tag{7}$$

pressure dependant of G

and for an isobaric process,

$$S = -\left(\frac{\partial G}{\partial T}\right)_P \tag{8}$$

temperature dependent of G

But from Gibbs free energy function,

$$G = E - TS + PV$$
$$= (E + PV) - TS$$

or, $\quad G = H - TS$

$$S = -\left(\frac{G-H}{T}\right) \tag{9}$$

From equations (8) and (9), we have

$$\left(\frac{\partial G}{\partial T}\right)_P = \left(\frac{G-H}{T}\right)$$

or $\quad H = G - T\left(\frac{\partial G}{\partial T}\right)_P \tag{10}$

Next,

$$\left[\frac{\partial}{\partial T}\left(\frac{G}{T}\right)\right]_P = -\frac{G}{T^2} + \frac{1}{T}\left(\frac{\partial G}{\partial T}\right)_P$$

$$\left[\frac{\partial}{\partial T}\left(\frac{G}{T}\right)\right]_P = -\frac{G}{T^2} + \frac{1}{T}\left(\frac{G-H}{T}\right)$$

$\therefore \quad H = -T^2\left[\frac{\partial}{\partial T}\left(\frac{G}{T}\right)\right]_P \tag{11}$

Equations (10) and (11) are known as Gibbs-Helmholtz equation.

Chapter 4. Mathematical theorems and thermodynamic relations

CHAPTER 4.
MATHEMATICAL THEOREMS AND THERMODYNAMIC RELATIONS

4.1 Mathematical theorem in partial differential calculus

Let there exist a function such that

$$f(x, y, z) = 0$$

Here x can be taken as function of y and z,

$$x = x(y, z)$$

$$\therefore \qquad dx = \left(\frac{\partial x}{\partial y}\right)_z dy + \left(\frac{\partial x}{\partial z}\right)_y dz \tag{1}$$

Similarly,

$$y = y(x, z)$$

$$\therefore \qquad dy = \left(\frac{\partial y}{\partial x}\right)_z dx + \left(\frac{\partial y}{\partial z}\right)_x dz \tag{2}$$

putting the expression of dy from equation (2) into (1), we get

$$dx = \left(\frac{\partial x}{\partial y}\right)_z \left[\left(\frac{\partial y}{\partial x}\right)_z dx + \left(\frac{\partial y}{\partial z}\right)_x dz\right] + \left(\frac{\partial x}{\partial z}\right)_y dz$$

$$dx = \left(\frac{\partial x}{\partial y}\right)_z \left(\frac{\partial y}{\partial x}\right)_z dx + \left[\left(\frac{\partial x}{\partial y}\right)_z \left(\frac{\partial y}{\partial z}\right)_x + \left(\frac{\partial x}{\partial z}\right)_y\right] dz \tag{3}$$

where out of the three coordinates only two variables are independent. If x & z are taken as the independent variables, eq.(3) must be true for all sets of values of dx and dz. If dz = 0, dx ≠ 0, it follows that

$$\left(\frac{\partial x}{\partial y}\right)_z \left(\frac{\partial y}{\partial x}\right)_z = 1$$

Therefore,

$$\left(\frac{\partial x}{\partial y}\right)_z = \frac{1}{\left(\frac{\partial y}{\partial x}\right)_z} \tag{4}$$

If $dx = 0$, $dz \neq 0$, it follows

$$\left(\frac{\partial x}{\partial y}\right)_z \left(\frac{\partial y}{\partial z}\right)_x + \left(\frac{\partial x}{\partial z}\right)_y = 0$$

using Eq. (4), we get

$$\left(\frac{\partial x}{\partial y}\right)_z \left(\frac{\partial y}{\partial z}\right)_x = -\left(\frac{\partial x}{\partial z}\right)_y$$

$$\left(\frac{\partial x}{\partial y}\right)_z \left(\frac{\partial y}{\partial z}\right)_x \left(\frac{\partial z}{\partial x}\right)_y = -1 \tag{5}$$

The above equations can be applied to thermodynamic systems,

(a) In case of PVT system, we can define

$$\left(\frac{\partial P}{\partial V}\right)_T \left(\frac{\partial V}{\partial T}\right)_P = -\left(\frac{\partial P}{\partial T}\right)_V$$

(b) $\beta = coefficient\ of\ volume\ expansion = \frac{1}{V}\left(\frac{\partial V}{\partial T}\right)_P$ and

$$\kappa = Isothermal\ compressibility = -\frac{1}{V}\left(\frac{\partial V}{\partial P}\right)_T$$

Therefore,

$$\frac{\beta}{\kappa} = \frac{\frac{1}{V}\left(\frac{\partial V}{\partial T}\right)_P}{-\frac{1}{V}\left(\frac{\partial V}{\partial P}\right)_T} = -\left(\frac{\partial V}{\partial T}\right)_P \left(\frac{\partial P}{\partial V}\right)_T = \left(\frac{\partial P}{\partial T}\right)_V$$

4.2 Heat capacities equations

From TdS equations, we have the following thermodynamic relationship (see section 4.6 and 4.7 of this chapter)

$$TdS = C_V dT + T\left(\frac{\partial P}{\partial T}\right)_V dV$$

$$TdS = C_P dT - T\left(\frac{\partial V}{\partial T}\right)_P dP$$

Equating the two equations, we get

$$C_P dT - T\left(\frac{\partial V}{\partial T}\right)_P dP = c_V dT + T\left(\frac{\partial P}{\partial T}\right)_V dV$$

Solving for dT, we get

$$dT = \frac{T\left(\frac{\partial P}{\partial T}\right)_V}{C_P - C_V} dV + \frac{T\left(\frac{\partial V}{\partial T}\right)_P}{C_P - C_V} dP \qquad (6)$$

But $\qquad\qquad$ T = T(V,P)

So, $\qquad dT = \left(\frac{\partial T}{\partial V}\right)_P dV + \left(\frac{\partial T}{\partial P}\right)_V dP \qquad (7)$

Comparing equations (6) and (7), we get

$$\left(\frac{\partial T}{\partial V}\right)_P = \frac{T\left(\frac{\partial P}{\partial T}\right)_V}{C_P - C_V} \qquad \text{and}$$

$$\left(\frac{\partial T}{\partial P}\right)_V = \frac{T\left(\frac{\partial V}{\partial T}\right)_P}{C_P - C_V}$$

Thus using equation (4), we get

$$C_P - C_V = \frac{T\left(\frac{\partial P}{\partial T}\right)_V}{\left(\frac{\partial T}{\partial V}\right)_P}$$

$$C_P - C_V = T\left(\frac{\partial P}{\partial T}\right)_V \left(\frac{\partial V}{\partial T}\right)_P \qquad (8)$$

but from PVT relation

$$\left(\frac{\partial P}{\partial V}\right)_T \left(\frac{\partial V}{\partial T}\right)_P = -\left(\frac{\partial P}{\partial T}\right)_V$$

Thus,

$$C_P - C_V = -T\left(\frac{\partial V}{\partial T}\right)_P^2 \left(\frac{\partial P}{\partial V}\right)_T \qquad (9)$$

4.3 First Internal energy equation

For a pure substance undergoing an infinitesimal reversible process between two equilibrium states, the change of internal energy will be given by

$$dU = TdS - PdV \tag{10}$$

or,
$$\frac{dU}{dV} = T\frac{dS}{dV} - P$$

where U, S and P are considered as functions of T and V. If T is constant

$$\left(\frac{\partial U}{\partial V}\right)_T = T\left(\frac{\partial S}{\partial V}\right)_T - P$$

Using Maxwell's 3rd relation

$$\left(\frac{\partial S}{\partial V}\right)_T = \left(\frac{\partial P}{\partial T}\right)_V$$

we get

$$\left(\frac{\partial U}{\partial V}\right)_T = T\left(\frac{\partial P}{\partial T}\right)_V - P \tag{11}$$

Equation (11) is known as first internal energy equation. This equation find many thermodynamic applications. For example in case of an Ideal gas, we have

$$PV = nRT$$

or,
$$P = \frac{nRT}{V}$$

$$\left(\frac{\partial P}{\partial T}\right)_V = \frac{nR}{V}$$

Therefore,

$$\left(\frac{\partial U}{\partial V}\right)_T = T\frac{nR}{V} - P = 0$$

Thus for an ideal gas, U does not depend on V but is a function of T only.

4.4 Second internal energy equation

From equation (10), we have

$$dU = TdS - PdV$$

$$\frac{dU}{dP} = T\frac{dS}{dP} - P\frac{dV}{dP}$$

where U, S and V are the functions of T and P.

If T is constant

$$\left(\frac{\partial U}{\partial P}\right)_T = T\left(\frac{\partial S}{\partial P}\right)_T - P\left(\frac{\partial V}{\partial P}\right)_T$$

But from Maxwell's 4th relation

$$\left(\frac{\partial S}{\partial P}\right)_T = -\left(\frac{\partial V}{\partial T}\right)_P$$

$$\left(\frac{\partial U}{\partial P}\right)_T = -T\left(\frac{\partial V}{\partial T}\right)_P - P\left(\frac{\partial V}{\partial P}\right)_T \tag{12}$$

Equation (12) is known as first internal energy equation.

4.5 Bulk modulus and coefficient of volume expansion

For a sound wave propagating in a medium, we have average bulk modulus is defined as

$$B = \frac{\text{change of pressure}}{\text{change in volume per unit volume}}$$

$$= \frac{\Delta P}{\left(\frac{\Delta V}{V}\right)} = V\left(\frac{\Delta P}{\Delta V}\right)$$

but for ΔP = positive, ΔV becomes negative and that describe a compression of the medium.

Therefore,

$$B = -V\left(\frac{\Delta P}{\Delta V}\right)$$

At constant temperature, isothermal bulk modulus can be defined as

$$B = -V\left(\frac{\partial P}{\partial V}\right)_T$$

and isothermal compressibility is given by

$$\kappa = \frac{1}{B} = -\frac{1}{V}\left(\frac{\partial V}{\partial P}\right)_T$$

The coefficient of volume expansion (β) can be defined as follows.

At constant pressure, we have

$$\beta = \frac{change\ in\ volume\ per\ unit\ volume}{change\ in\ temp}$$

$$= \frac{\left(\frac{\Delta V}{V}\right)}{\Delta T} = \frac{1}{V}\left(\frac{\Delta V}{\Delta T}\right)_P$$

For a infinitesimal change in temperature, i.e;

$$\Delta T \rightarrow \partial T$$

$$\Delta V \rightarrow \partial V$$

The coefficient of volume expansion or volume expansivity can be defined as

$$\beta = \frac{1}{V}\left(\frac{\partial V}{\partial T}\right)_P$$

4.6 First TdS relation

The entropy of a substance can be considered as a function of any two variables, such as the T and V.

$$S = S(T, V)$$

Therefore,

$$dS = \left(\frac{\partial S}{\partial T}\right)_V dT + \left(\frac{\partial S}{\partial V}\right)_T dV$$

or, $\qquad TdS = T\left(\frac{\partial S}{\partial T}\right)_V dT + T\left(\frac{\partial S}{\partial V}\right)_T dV \qquad\qquad (13)$

But for a reversible isochoric process (dV = 0),

$$TdS = dQ$$

and $$T\left(\frac{\partial S}{\partial T}\right)_V = \left(\frac{dQ}{dT}\right)_V = C_V$$

and from Maxwell's 3rd relation,

$$\left(\frac{\partial S}{\partial V}\right)_T = \left(\frac{\partial P}{\partial T}\right)_V$$

Substituting into equation (14), we get

$$TdS = C_V dT + T\left(\frac{\partial P}{\partial T}\right)_V dV \qquad (14)$$

Example 1. Calculate the amount of heat transferred when 1 mol of a Van der waals gas undergoes a reversible isothermal expansion from an initial molar volume v_i to a final molar volume v_f.

For 1 mol of a Van der Waals gas, we have

$$Tds = c_v dT + T\left(\frac{\partial P}{\partial T}\right)_v dv$$

Where s, v and c_v are molar quantities. Using molar Van der Waals equation of state, we get

$$P = \frac{RT}{v-b} - \frac{a}{v^2}$$

So, $$\left(\frac{\partial P}{\partial T}\right)_V = \frac{R}{v-b}$$

$$\therefore \quad Tds = c_v dT + \frac{TR}{v-b} dv$$

Since T is a constant, $c_v dT = 0$ and since the process is reversible, the heat transferred during the process

$$q = \int Tds$$

$$q = RT \int_{v_i}^{v_f} \frac{dv}{v-b} = RT\ln\left(\frac{v_f-b}{v_i-b}\right)$$

4.7 Second TdS relation

The entropy of a pure substance can also be functions of T and P. Let

$$S = S(T, P)$$

$$dS = \left(\frac{\partial S}{\partial T}\right)_P dT + \left(\frac{\partial S}{\partial P}\right)_T dP$$

Thus

$$TdS = T\left(\frac{\partial S}{\partial T}\right)_P dT + T\left(\frac{\partial S}{\partial P}\right)_T dP$$

But
$$T\left(\frac{\partial S}{\partial T}\right)_P = C_P$$

and from Maxwell's 4th relation

$$\left(\frac{\partial S}{\partial P}\right)_T = -\left(\frac{\partial V}{\partial T}\right)_P$$

Therefore, we have

$$TdS = c_p dT - T\left(\frac{\partial V}{\partial T}\right)_P dP \tag{15}$$

In terms of the volume expension,

$$\beta = \frac{1}{V}\left(\frac{\partial V}{\partial T}\right)_P$$

Equation (15) becomes

$$TdS = C_p dT - T\beta V dP \tag{16}$$

Example 2. Reversible isothermal change of pressure

When T is constant, we have from equation (15) and (16)

$$TdS = -T\left(\frac{\partial V}{\partial T}\right)_P dP = -T\beta V dP$$

Therefore

$$Q = -T \int \left(\frac{\partial V}{\partial T}\right)_P dP$$

$$= -T \int \beta V dP, \; since \; dQ = -TdS$$

For most of the solids and liquids, β and V is supposed to be constant (with respect of P)

$$\therefore \qquad Q = -TV\beta \int_{P_i}^{P_f} dP$$

$$Q = -TV\beta(P_f - P_i)$$

From this equation, one can see that as the pressure is increased isothermally, Q is negative. That is, heat will flow out if β is positive. But for a substance with β negative (such as water at 0°C and 4 °C or a rubber band), an isothermal increase of pressure causes an absorption of heat.

4.8 Difference in heat capacities

From equation (9), we have

$$C_P - C_V = -T\left(\frac{\partial V}{\partial T}\right)_P^2 \left(\frac{\partial P}{\partial V}\right)_T \qquad (17)$$

For an ideal gas, we have

$$PV = nRT$$

$$\left(\frac{\partial V}{\partial T}\right)_P = \frac{nR}{P} = \frac{V}{T}$$

$$\left(\frac{\partial P}{\partial V}\right)_T = -\frac{nRT}{V^2}$$

Thus from equation (17), we have

$$C_P - C_V = +T\frac{V^2}{T^2}\frac{nRT}{V^2}$$

$$C_P - C_V = nR$$

Eq(17) can be expressed in terms of volume expansivity (β)

$$\beta = \frac{1}{V}\left(\frac{\partial V}{\partial T}\right)_P$$

and Isothermal compressibility (κ)

$$\kappa_T = -\frac{1}{V}\left(\frac{\partial V}{\partial P}\right)_T$$

Therefore,

$$C_P - C_V = \frac{TV\left[\frac{1}{V}\left(\frac{\partial V}{\partial T}\right)_P\right]^2}{-\frac{1}{V}\left(\frac{\partial V}{\partial P}\right)_T}$$

and

$$C_P - C_V = \frac{TV\beta^2}{\kappa_T} \tag{18}$$

4.9 Ratio of heat capacities

The TdS equations for specific heats are given by Eq. (14) and (15)

$$TdS = C_P dT - T\left(\frac{\partial V}{\partial T}\right)_P dP$$

$$TdS = C_V dT + T\left(\frac{\partial P}{\partial T}\right)_V dV$$

At constant S,

$$C_P dT_s = T\left(\frac{\partial V}{\partial T}\right)_P dP_s$$

$$C_V dT_s = -T\left(\frac{\partial P}{\partial T}\right)_V dV_s$$

$$\therefore \quad \frac{C_P}{C_V} = -\left[\left(\frac{\partial V}{\partial T}\right)_P \Big/ \left(\frac{\partial P}{\partial T}\right)_V\right]\left(\frac{\partial P}{\partial V}\right)_S$$

$$=-\left[\left(\frac{\partial V}{\partial T}\right)_P\left(\frac{\partial T}{\partial P}\right)_V\right]\left(\frac{\partial P}{\partial V}\right)_S$$

$$\frac{C_P}{C_V}=-\left(\frac{\partial V}{\partial P}\right)_T\left(\frac{\partial P}{\partial V}\right)_S$$

Thus
$$\frac{C_P}{C_V}=\gamma=\frac{\left(\frac{\partial P}{\partial V}\right)_S}{\left(\frac{\partial P}{\partial V}\right)_T}\tag{19}$$

The adiabatic or isentropic compressibility (κ_s) is

$$\kappa_s=-\frac{1}{V}\left(\frac{\partial V}{\partial P}\right)_S$$

Now

$$\frac{\kappa_T}{\kappa_s}=\frac{-\frac{1}{V}\left(\frac{\partial V}{\partial P}\right)_T}{-\frac{1}{V}\left(\frac{\partial V}{\partial P}\right)_S}$$

Using the theorem

$$\left(\frac{\partial x}{\partial y}\right)_z=\frac{1}{\left(\frac{\partial y}{\partial x}\right)_z}$$

We get

$$\frac{\kappa_T}{\kappa_s}=\frac{\left(\frac{\partial P}{\partial V}\right)_S}{\left(\frac{\partial P}{\partial V}\right)_T}=\gamma$$

$$\gamma=\frac{\kappa_T}{\kappa_s}\tag{20}$$

Chapter 5. Phase transitions and critical phenomena

CHAPTER 5.
PHASE TRANSITIONS AND CRITICAL PHENOMENA

5.1 Gibbs function G(P,T)

Gibbs function can be defined as,

$$G=E+PV-TS$$

or,
$$G=H-TS$$

For an infinitesimal reversible process,

$$dG=dE+PdV+VdP-TdS-SdT$$

but from 1st law

$$dE=TdS-PdV$$

Thus,
$$dG=TdS-PdV+PdV+VdP-TdS-SdT$$

$$dG=VdP-SdT \tag{1}$$

$$G=G(P,T)$$

$$dG = \left(\frac{\partial G}{\partial P}\right)_T dP + \left(\frac{\partial G}{\partial T}\right)_P dT \tag{2}$$

Comparing equations (1) and (2), we get

$$V = \left(\frac{\partial G}{\partial P}\right)_T$$

$$-S = \left(\frac{\partial G}{\partial T}\right)_P \tag{3}$$

so the volume and entropy may be calculated by the partial differentiation.

In the case of reversible isothermal and isobaric process, we have from equation (1)

$$dG = 0$$

$$G = \text{constant}$$

as $dT = 0$ and $dP = 0$

This result is in connection with the processes involving a change of phase. The processes such as sublimation (solid to vapor), fusion (solid to liquid) and vaporization (liquid to vapor) takes place isothermally and isobarically. During such processes the Gibbs function remains constant.

5.2 First order phase transition: Clausius Clapeyron equation

During the first order phase transition such as the melting (fusion), vaporization (boiling) and sublimation, the temperature and pressure remain constant while the entropy and the volume change.

Consider n_0 moles of a material contained in phase I where, s^i is the molar entropy and v^i the molar volume. One can write from equation (3),

$$s^i = - \left(\frac{\partial g^{(i)}}{\partial T} \right)_P$$

$$v^i = \left(\frac{\partial g^{(i)}}{\partial P} \right)_T \tag{4}$$

The quantities, s^i and v^i have been as functions of T and P. During the phase transition of the material from phase i to the phase f, thermodynamic quantities, the T and P remain constant.

Now if x is the fraction of the initial phase that was transformed into the final phase at any moment. Then the entropy S and the volume V of the mixture at any moment are given by

$$S = n_o(1 - x)s^i + n_o x s^f$$

$$V = n_o(1 - x)v^i + n_o x v^f$$

where the quantities, s^f and v^f were defined as the molar entropy and molar volume of the material in phase f.

$$s^f = -\left(\frac{\partial g^{(f)}}{\partial T}\right)_P$$

$$v^f = \left(\frac{\partial g^{(f)}}{\partial P}\right)_T \tag{5}$$

Suppose the phase transition takes place reversibly at constant pressure, the change of enthalpy per mole is then given by

$$\Delta h = h^f - h^i = T\Delta S = T(s^f - s^i) \tag{6}$$

as $dH = TdS + VdP$ and at constant P, $dH = TdS$

Thus there is a change of molar entropy during the transition. Considering the above equations, one can characterize the first order phase transition by the following statements

(a) There are changes of molar entropy and molar volume.

(b) The first order derivatives of the molar Gibbs function change discontinuity $\left(\frac{\partial g}{\partial T} \text{ or } \frac{\partial g}{\partial P} \neq 0\right)$.

Fig (1) shows the variation of g (molar Gibbs function), s (molar entropy), v(molar volume) and c_p (molar heat capacity) at constant P. It shows a reversible phase change from liquid to vapor.

From fig 1(a), one can observe that the molar Gibbs function has a single value at the vaporization temperature, but the slope is discontinuous. As can be seen from fig 1(d), during the transition the molar heat capacity of a mixture of two phases is infinite.

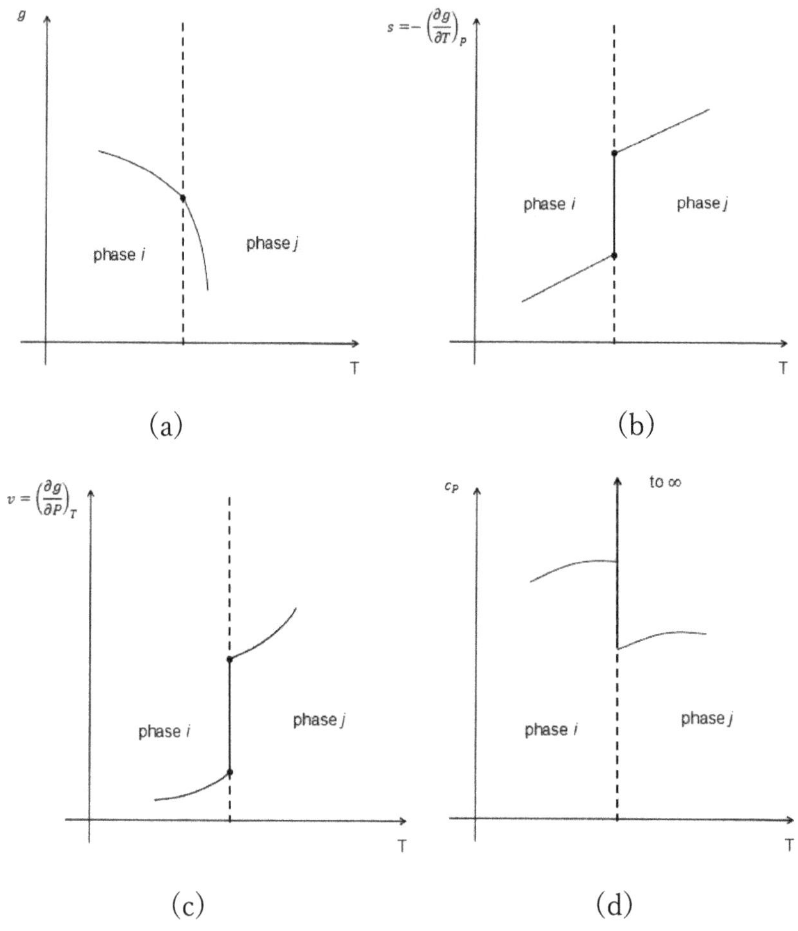

Fig 1. Characterization of a first order phase transition. (a) molar Gibbs function, (b) molar entropy, (c) molar volume, and (d) molar heat capacity.

Here the transition occurs at constant T and P and when P is constant, dT= 0 or when T is constant, dP= 0

$$\therefore c_p = T\left(\frac{\partial S}{\partial T}\right)_P \to \infty$$

Similarly,
$$\beta = \frac{1}{v}\,T\left(\frac{\partial v}{\partial T}\right)_P \to \infty$$

and
$$\kappa = -\frac{1}{v}\,T\left(\frac{\partial v}{\partial p}\right)_T \to \infty$$

This is valid only when the two phases co-exist.

5.3 Clausius Clapeyron equation

We know that the Gibbs function is a constant during any reversible process taking place at constant temperature and pressure. Thus for a phase change occurring at a temperature, T and a pressure, P, we have

$$g^i = g^f$$

And for a phase change taking place at temperature of (T+dT) and pressure, (P+dP)

$$g^i + dg^i = g^f + dg^f$$

Subtracting, we get

$$dg^i = dg^f$$

Now using equations (4) and (5), we get

$$-s^i dT + \vartheta^i dP = -s^f dT + \vartheta^f dP$$

$$\left(\vartheta^f - \vartheta^i\right)dP = \left(s^f - s^i\right)dT$$

$$\frac{dP}{dT} = \frac{\left(s^f - s^i\right)}{\left(\vartheta^f - \vartheta^i\right)}$$

$$= \frac{l}{T(\vartheta^f - \vartheta^i)} \tag{7}$$

But from equation (6)

$$\left(s^f - s^i\right) = \frac{h^f - h^i}{T} = \frac{l}{T}$$

where the difference in molar enthalpies at a constant pressure represents the molar latent heat.

Therefore

$$\frac{dP}{dT} = \frac{h^f - h^i}{T(\vartheta^f - \vartheta^i)} \tag{8}$$

The equations (7) and (8) are known as Clausius–Clapeyron equation.

5.4 Second order phase transition

There are some phase transitions during which there is no transfer of heat and no change of volume. Such as the transition from liquid He 1 to liquid He 2. These transition are called second order phase transition.

We have observed that during the first order phase transition, the molar entropy $s = -\left(\frac{\partial g}{\partial T}\right)_P$ and the molar volume $v = \left(\frac{\partial g}{\partial P}\right)_T$ are discontinuous at the transition point.

The second order phase transition is however continues and during the transition, the molar entropy and molar volume remains the same at the end of the transitions. On the other hand, second order phase transitions are the phenomenon that takes place with no change in entropy and volume at constant temperature & pressure. Followings are some of the examples of second order phase transition:

transition of liquid He 1 to liquid He 2, transition of ferromagnetism to paramagnetism at curie point temperature, the transition super conductivity to normal conductivity in zero magnetic field, and order–disorder transitions in chemical compounds & alloys.

5.5 Ehrenfest equations

For a second order phase transition, there is no change in entropy and volume. Thus we have

(a) $$s^{(i)} = s^{(f)}$$ at (T, P)

and

$$s^{(i)} + ds^{(i)} = s^{(f)} + ds^{(f)}$$ at (T+dT,P+dP)

$\therefore$ $$ds^{(i)} = ds^{(f)} \qquad (9)$$

Since, $$s = s(T, P)$$

$$ds = \left(\frac{\partial s}{\partial T}\right)_P dT + \left(\frac{\partial s}{\partial P}\right)_T dP$$

$$= \left(\frac{c_p}{T}\right) dT + \left(\frac{\partial s}{\partial P}\right)_T dP$$

But from Maxwell's equation

$$\left(\frac{\partial s}{\partial P}\right)_T = -\left(\frac{\partial v}{\partial T}\right)_P$$

And $\quad \frac{1}{v}\left(\frac{\partial v}{\partial T}\right)_P = \beta$, coefficient of volume expansion

Thus $$ds = \left(\frac{c_p}{T}\right) dT - \left(\frac{\partial v}{\partial T}\right)_P dP$$

$$ds = \left(\frac{c_p}{T}\right) dT - \vartheta\beta dP$$

Now from (9)

$$\left(\frac{c_p^{(i)}}{T}\right)dT - v\beta^{(i)}dP = \left(\frac{c_p^{(f)}}{T}\right)dT - v\beta^{(f)}dP$$

on rearranging, we get

$$\left(\frac{dP}{dT}\right) = \left(\frac{1}{Tv}\right)\frac{c^{(f)}-c^{(i)}}{\beta^{(f)}-\beta^{(i)}} \tag{10}$$

(b) Again,

$$v^{(i)} = v^{(f)} \qquad \text{at constant (T, P)}$$

and $\quad v^{(i)} + dv^{(i)} = v^{(f)} + dv^{(f)} \qquad at\ (T+dT, P+dP)$

Therefore,

$$dv^{(i)} = dv^{(f)} \tag{11}$$

Now, $\qquad v = v(T, P)$

So, $\qquad dv = \left(\frac{\partial \vartheta}{\partial T}\right)_P dT + \left(\frac{\partial \vartheta}{\partial P}\right)_T dP$

$$dv = v\beta dT - v\kappa dP \tag{12}$$

Where we have used expressions for the coefficient of volume expansion and the coefficient of isothermal compressibility

$$\frac{1}{v}\left(\frac{\partial v}{\partial T}\right)_P = \beta,\ and\ \kappa = -\frac{1}{v}\left(\frac{\partial v}{\partial P}\right)_T$$

Thus from equation (11), one can write

$$v\beta^{(i)}dT - v\kappa^{(i)}dP = v\beta^{(f)}dT - v\kappa^{(f)}dP$$

$$\left(\beta^{(f)} - \beta^{(i)}\right)dT = \left(\kappa^{(f)} - \kappa^{(i)}\right)dP$$

Therefore,

$$\frac{dP}{dT} = \frac{\left(\beta^{(f)} - \beta^{(i)}\right)}{\left(\kappa^{(f)} - \kappa^{(i)}\right)} \tag{13}$$

Equations (10) and (13) are known as the Ehrenfest equations.

Index

Recommended Books

1. Thermal Physics, Kittel and Kroemer, W. H. Freeman; Second Edition (1980).

2. Introduction to Thermal Physics, D. Schroeder, Pearson (1999).

3. Thermal Physics: with Kinetic Theory, Thermodynamics and Statistical Mechanics, S.C. Garg , R.M. Bansal, C.K. Ghosh, Tata McGraw Hill Education Private Limited; 2e Edition (2013).

4. Thermal Physics: An Introduction to Thermodynamics, Statistical Mechanics and Kinetic Theory, P.C. Riedi, Macmillan (1976).

5. A Treatise on Heat, Meghnad Saha, and B.N. Srivastava, Indian Press (1969).

6. Thermodynamics, Enrico Fermi, Courier Dover Publications (1956).

7. Thermodynamics, Kinetic theory & Statistical thermodynamics, F.W.Sears & G.L.Salinger, Narosa (1988).

8. Thermal Physics by Satya Prakash and J. P. Agarwal, Pragati Prakashan (2012).

9. Heat and Thermodynamics, Zeemansky and R. H. Dittman, Tata McGraw Hill (1997).

10. Thermodynamics, Zeemansky, Tata McGraw Hill, 5th Edition (1968).